ask the kids

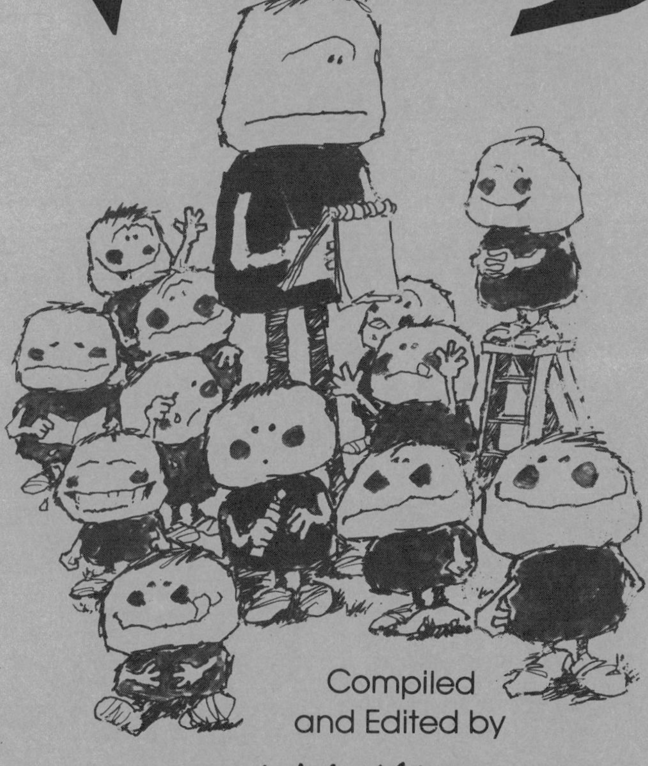

Compiled and Edited by

Pat McKissack

Illustrated by Larry Thomas

Publishing House
St. Louis

To My Children

Copyright © 1981
Concordia Publishing House
3558 South Jefferson Avenue
Saint Louis, Missouri 63118

Manufactured in the United States of America

Unless otherwise stated, the Scripture quotations in this publication are from the Revised Standard Version of the Bible, coyrighted 1946, 1952, © 1971, 1973 by the Division of Christian Education of the National Council of the Churches of Christ in the U.S.A., and used by permission.

1 2 3 4 5 6 7 8 9 10 CPC 90 89 88 87 86 85 84 83 82 81

McKissack, Patricia C., 1944-
    Ask the kids.

    1. Children—Religious life. I. Title.
BV4571.2.M36   230'.088054   81-1614
ISBN 0-570-04057-4

AACR2

CONTENTS

Introduction	4
How Old Is God?	6
What Does God Look Like?	8
Is God Dead?	10
If You Could Ask God to Change One Thing, What Would It Be?	12
How Is God Like a Father?	14
Can You Hide Anything from God?	16
Does God Know What You're Thinking?	18
How Did God Create the World?	20
What Is Your Favorite Thing That God Made?	22
Where Is Heaven? What Is It Like?	24
Who Is Jesus Christ?	26
Where Was Jesus Born?	28
What Is Your Favorite Christmas Carol?	30
What Were the Three Gifts of the Wise Men? Do You Know What These Gifts Were?	32
What Did Jesus Mean When He Said "Love Your Neighbor?"	34
What Is a Parable?	36
How Do You Feel About Judas?	38
What Does Resurrection Mean?	40
Are You a Christian?	42
Who Is the Holy Ghost?	44
What Is Sin?	46
If a Person Sins, and You See Him or Her, What Would You Do?	48
What Do You Think of the Devil?	50
Which One of the Ten Commandments Do You See Other People Breaking the Most?	52
What Does "Taking the Lord's Name in Vain" Mean?	54
What Is an Atheist?	56
What Do You Like Best About Church Service?	58
How Do You Pray?	60
What Is Your Favorite Prayer?	62
What Is an Angel?	64
What Is a Miracle?	66
Do You Read the Bible?	68
Who Is Your Favorite Bible Character and Why?	70
Finish This Poem . . .	72

INTRODUCTION

I imagine when Jesus received the children it had a humbling effect on the adults around Him. In those days children were to be seen and not heard, but Jesus knew the minds and hearts of little children.

"Let the children come to Me," He said. And I'm sure they came, running, laughing, bursting with joy. He welcomed them; He touched them. The younger ones probably crawled on His lap and hugged His neck, while the older children sat wide-eyed at His feet.

Jesus' message was one of love, and children give and receive love so generously; I'm sure each child accepted His message openly, freely, and with no reservations. I believe it was the children's pure and simple acceptance that prompted Him to say, " . . . for to such belongs the kingdom of heaven."

Children today can't actually see and touch Jesus, but it is evident from the contents of this book that the same uninhibited acceptance of His message is still very real.

This project began three years ago in a New York bus station. Scrawled across a wall in black spray paint was the disheartening message "GOD IS DEAD." A little girl sitting next to me, who was about five or six years old, pulled my sleeve and asked, "Miss Lady, what do those letters say?" Reluctantly, I told her, but quickly asked, "Do you think God is dead?" Her response was quick and to the point. "Oh, no, God isn't dead. He's God, and God can't die!" She was not the slightest bit intimidated by the words or the thoughts behind them. It was unthinkable to her that God could die, and frankly, I was amazed by such faith in one so young.

That one incident started me on a venture that has brought me many pleasant and enlightening hours with children in parochial schools, Sunday schools, and vacation Bible schools all over the country. As an adult Christian, I have been deeply moved by the simple yet profound answers children have given to rather difficult questions about their religion. For me, Ask the Kids has been an affirmation that out of the mouths of babes often come pearls of wisdom . . . and, unfortunately, gross misunderstandings!

To young children, religion is a gigantic puzzle with numerous pieces spread out before them. Putting the puzzle together is an awesome task which they cannot (should not) be allowed to tackle alone. Many times children will put a puzzle piece in the wrong place. It is the careful guidance of adults that helps children through the various stages of spiritual growth and development so that the end result will be one of true understanding and sound application of the basic Christian principles.

This book is "by children" but not "for children!" Although the illustrations are light and humorous, this is not a children's book. Those who know today's child, teach, and work with them will appreciate the answers as a measure of where their charges "might" be in their understanding and will know how to plan for reaching them with the fundamental truths.

All the children questioned had some religious training in a formal setting, yet without exception, from the youngest to the oldest child, I found misconceptions, conflicts with Scripture, or general lack of knowledge. In no way does this reflect on the teachers involved. I found that there were two reasons for the problems. Basic concepts (God the Creator, Jesus the Savior) are taught early, but concepts like the Trinity and forgiveness, etc. are taught much later on. Nevertheless, children are exposed to the terms and then left to their own interpretations, which often result in misunderstandings. This can hardly be helped. Second, there is so much to learn, so many concepts to understand, that no one teacher or parent can cover them all in the limited time allowed.

This book gives you, the parent, teacher, or adult a glimpse at what our children are thinking, at what age, and more importantly, what we "must" do to help them put the pieces together properly.

If you are a parent, ask your children some of the questions and listen to the responses. You can learn quite a bit about where your child is in his or her spiritual growth and development by listening to them tell you their feelings about God, Jesus, and Christianity in general.

If you are a Sunday school teacher or religion instructor, you might want to use some of these questions or answers as discussion starters, introductions to lessons, or writing assignments.

Ask yourself some of the questions. What are the answers? Can you, like a child, accept the invitation to "come unto Me"?

Read. Enjoy. Reflect. Respond. Be a child, for "to such belongs the kingdom of heaven."

How old is God?

God is as old as anything... everything.

Beth, age 8

God is super old. More old than anybody alive.

Mackie, age 8

God is old-old.

Harry, age 8

God and my grandfather are about the same age.

Charles, age 6

God doesn't have a birthday because He was never born. He has always been.

Gene, age 10

WHAT DOES GOD LOOK LIKE?

God is bright like the sun.

Jessica, age 7

God looks like Mr. Windsor, what lives down the street. He looks just like God would look to me. But Mr. Windsor sure ain't God. God wouldn't run kids off His grass.

Leroi, age 8

God looks like...well...like an old man, but He isn't old. You know what I mean? God can't get old and die and stuff.

Michael age 8

God is a spirit and doesn't have a body. You just feel God because you can't see Him like you do people.

Lawrence, age 10

IS GOD DEAD?

No, God isn't dead, but He's very old.

Lynn, age 6

God isn't dead. He's God, and God can't die.

Jamie, age 6

I wouldn't ask questions like that if I were you, Mrs. McKissack.

Sammy, age 7

God wouldn't do a thing like that! (Like what?) Like die!

Alexander, age 6

If God died, Jesus would still be around to protect us. (How do you know?) Because, Jesus died already, and came back to life again.

Pete, age 8

God will live forever. He can't die.

Billy, age 8

Thy name, O Lord, endures forever, Thy renown, O Lord, throughout all ages.

Psalm 135:13

IF YOU COULD ASK GOD TO CHANGE ONE THING, WHAT WOULD IT BE?

I'd like to change a lot of stuff, but I can't. (What if you could?) If I really could, I'd ask God to do away with being little. (Little or young?) Young, like seven or eight years old. I think you should not be born, but just grown. It's hard to explain, but if I could, I'd ask never to be young.
I'd ask to have our bodies changed. Everyone would be perfect. If someone lost a leg or an eye, it would just grow back. Wouldn't that be great?

Marvin, age 8

God did it all right the first time; it was the people who messed it up. I'd ask that God have fewer people.

Hanna, age 8

I would ask God to make it hot in cold places and cold in hot places. That way it would be hot in my city instead of cold.

Lynn, age 7

God loves righteousness and justice; the earth is full of the steadfast love of the Lord.

Psalm 33:5

HOW IS GOD LIKE A FATHER?

God is like a father because
He takes care of you.

> Carolyn, age 8

God is like a father because
if you're good, then He is happy,
but if you are bad, He doesn't
like it too much.

> Lynn, age 12

God is like a father because
He sees everything you do.

> Lee, age 12

He (God) helps you and wants
you to grow up strong and
good, just like my father.

> Mickey, age 7

God is like a father 'cause we
are His children.

> Janice, age 12

Yet, O Lord, Thou art our Father; we are the clay, and Thou art our Potter; we all are the work of Thy hand.

> Isaiah 64:8

CAN YOU HIDE ANYTHING FROM GOD?

Nope!

                          Sammy, age 7

If you hide something in a drawer, God will see it.

                          Pete, age 6

You can't hide things from God, and it would be silly to try.

                          Aggie, age 8

I don't want to hide anything from God. It's my mother; she doesn't want me to keep things in the house. (Like what?) **Like bugs and spiders and things. God knows I have them, but Mom doesn't.**

                          Kevin, age 10

The eyes of the Lord are in every place, keeping watch on the evil and the good.

                          Proverbs 15:3

DOES GOD KNOW WHAT YOU'RE THINKING?

Um-m-m, that's a hard one. I guess so, He knows everything else.

Sammy, age 7

They say He knows what you're thinking and everything.

Jeannie, age 8

God can't... yes, He can. Mrs. King says God can do ANYTHING. So I guess He can know what you're thinking too. Whao!

Amy, age 7

O Lord, Thou hast searched me and known me!
Thou knowest when I sit down and when I rise up;
                    Thou discernest my thoughts from afar.
Thou searchest out my path and my lying down,
                    and art acquainted with all my ways.
Even before a word is on my tongue,
                    lo, O Lord, Thou knowest it altogether.

Psalm 139:1-4

How did God create the world?

It took God six days and He slept on the seventh day.

Helena, age 8

God created things, then animals, then people. Then He rested.

Peter, age 8

God did it all with no trouble at all.

Mickey, age 7

God said, "Let there..." and there was.

Angie, age 9

Thou art the Lord, Thou alone; Thou hast made heaven, the heaven of heavens, with all their host, the earth and all that is on it, the seas and all that is in them; and Thou preservest all of them; and the host of heaven worships Thee.

Nehemiah 9:6

WHAT IS YOUR FAVORITE THING THAT GOD MADE?

THE SUN!!!

Angela, age 7

I'm glad God made people.

Beth, age 8

I'm glad God made the trees and mountains, and rivers and oceans. He made them for us to enjoy.

Jessica, age 7

The best thing God made was boys! (Boo!) *Okay, okay, and girls too, but He made boys <u>first</u>.* (Boo!)

Harry, age 8

The heavens are telling the glory of God; and the firmament proclaims His handiwork. Day to day pours forth speech, and night to night declares knowledge.

Psalm 19:1-2

WHERE IS HEAVEN? WHAT IS IT LIKE?

Heaven is wherever God is.

> Sharron, age 10

You can't see heaven, even with a telescope. But it's there. I know it!

> Wally, age 9

That's simple... Heaven is God's house. It is clean and shining. People have plenty of food and no worries. It is a nice place to be, but it's hard to get there.

> Gloria, age 8

Heaven is where Grandpa and Grandma live now.

> Angie, age 5

Heaven is where God is and Jesus is too. When we die we can go there if we believe Jesus is our Savior.

> Sharon, age 10

WHO IS JESUS CHRIST?

Jesus is God.

Haley, age 11

Jesus is the Son of God.

Charles, age 9

Jesus is my Friend, and He takes care of me and everybody. He is very, very good and would never hurt anybody.

Lynn, age 6

Jesus is God's Son. He died on a cross and came back to life again. I learned that in Sunday school.

Bobby, age 8

Jesus is in heaven and lives with God. He is very good.

Marcia, age 6

Jesus said to them, "But who do you say I am?"
Simon Peter replied, "You are the Christ, the Son of the living God." And Jesus answered him, "Blessed are you, Simon Bar-Jona! For flesh and blood has not revealed this to you, but My Father who is in heaven."

Matthew 16:15-17

Jesus was born in Bethlehem.

Lonnie, age 8

Jesus was born in a stable in Bethlehem.

David, age 8

Jesus was born in Bethlehem a long time ago.

Hank, age 7

Jesus was born in heaven, and they sent Him down on a star.

Lawrence, age 4

Over there (pointing to nowhere in particular).

Ginny, age 4

And you, O Bethlehem, in the land of Judah, are by no means least among the rulers of Judah; for from you shall come a Ruler who will govern My people Israel.

Matthew 2:6

To you is born this day in the city of David a Savior, who is Christ the Lord.

Luke 2:11

WHAT IS YOUR FAVORITE CHRISTMAS CAROL?

I like "O Little Town of Bethlehem."

Jan, age 7

I like the one that goes, "Hark, the 'Harold' Angels sing-g-g-g."

Leroi, age 8

I like "Away in a Manger"... and "Silent Night"... and "O Little Town of Bethlehem"... and...

Grace, age 8

I like them all. We sing them all on Christmas Eve.

Jan, age 7

And suddenly there was with the angel a multitude of the heavenly host praising God and saying, "Glory to God in the highest and on earth peace among men with whom He is pleased."

Luke 2:13-14

WHAT WERE THE THREE GIFTS OF THE WISE MEN? DO YOU KNOW WHAT THESE GIFTS WERE?

Jesus was a king, and they (the Wise Men) gave Him gifts that were fit for a king.

Lynn, age 12

I know what gold is, but the other things (frankincense and myrrh) were just nice things to give to Jesus, I guess.

Marsha, age 8

Gold is easy, but those other two things are old-timey things that people don't use any more.

Amy, age 8

I'm not sure, but I think they were sweet-smelling things that people used in that time. The gold was money in those days.

Lee, age 12

And going into the house they saw the Child with Mary His mother, and they (the Wise Men) fell down and worshiped Him. Then, opening their treasures, they offered Him gifts, gold and frankincense and myrrh.

Matthew 2:11

WHAT DID JESUS MEAN WHEN HE SAID "LOVE YOUR NEIGHBOR?"

I don't know, but I don't love my neighbor, 'cause she's always picking on me, but I try to like her...sometimes.
— Alexander, age 6

It means that you are supposed to love people all around you.
— Charles, age 9

It means that if people live near you, you are supposed to love them, I guess...
— Alexander, age 6

You should love everybody no matter what because Jesus said so.
— Beverly, age 9

You are supposed to love people even if you don't know them.
— Johnny, age 10

By this all men will know that you are My disciples, if you have love for one another.
John 13:35

This is My commandment, that you love one another as I have loved you.
John 15:12

WHAT IS A PARABLE?

36

A parable is a story Jesus told about a boy who ran away, and a good Samaritan, too.

Lynn, age 10

A parable is a Jesus Bible story.

Carl, age 8

Jesus told stories, and they were called parables.

Kevin, age 8

Bible story books have parables. I have one at home.

Pam, age 6

With many such parables He spoke the Word to them, as they were able to hear it; He did not speak to them without a parable, but privately to His own disciples He explained everything.

Mark 4:33-34

HOW DO YOU FEEL ABOUT JUDAS?

Judas was bad because he told on Jesus and got Him (Jesus) killed.

Leroi, age 8

Judas kissed Jesus and gave Him away to the police. That was a dirty, mean thing to do.

Amy, age 7

I don't know why they even put Judas in the Bible.

Jessica, age 7

Judas told on his friend, and I don't think Jesus would have told on him (Judas).

Michael, age 8

While He was still speaking, Judas came, one of the Twelve, and with him a great crowd with swords and clubs, from the chief priests and the elders of the people. Now the betrayer had given them a sign, saying, "The one I shall kiss is the Man; seize Him." And he came up to Jesus at once and said, "Hail, Master!" And he kissed Him.

Matthew 26:47-49

WHAT DOES RESURRECTION MEAN?

Rest-tur-Rection means Easter. Jesus came alive again after they killed Him.

Jeannie, age 9

Res...res...that big word... has to do with Jesus. Some people killed Jesus and put Him in a cemetery. But Jesus came alive again and suprised everybody!

Toni, age 7

My mother said that that word meant that Jesus came alive after everybody thought He was dead. Now we can be forgiven for our sins. She said that was the imporant thing to remember.

Kevin, age 8

That's a big word. I can't say it because I don't know how, but I know what it means. (What?) It means God and Jesus are alive and living in heaven.

Marva, age 6

Jesus said to her, "I am the Resurrection and the Life; he who believes in Me, though he die, yet shall he live."

John 11:25

ARE YOU A CHRISTIAN?

I'm learning to be one.
> Michael, age 10

I'm a Christian because I believe in Jesus and that He is my Savior and the Savior of the world. Nobody didn't tell me that's what I should say; I really believe it on my own.
> Paul, age 12

I'm a Christian because I'm an American.
> Lance, age 7

I'm not sure I'm a Christian yet. I think there are a few more steps to go before I'm a full-fledged Christian.
> Janine, age 10

Being a Christian is not hard; all you have to do is just believe that Jesus is your Savior, and just like that – you're a Christian. It doesn't hurt or nothing.
> Philip, age 10

WHO IS THE HOLY GHOST?

Is the Holy Ghost the same as Holy Spirit? If so, then that's God.

Brenda, age 9

The Holy Ghost is not like other ghosts. He's in heaven and He doesn't scare people like other ghosts. He protects us. At least that's what I think it is.

JoAnn, age 8

The Holy Ghost is one of the three things God is. Father, Son, and Holy Ghost. We always say Holy Spirit though.
Holy Ghost is Jesus' ghost. When Jesus came alive again, He was a holy ghost.

Janna, age 10

The Holy Ghost is a special ghost. Not a Halloween ghost, but a very special part of church and religion.

Missy, age 7

(Christ said:) "These things I have spoken to you, while I am still with you. But the Counselor, the Holy Spirit, whom the Father will send in My name, He will teach you all things, and bring to your remembrance all that I have said to you."

John 14:25-26

WHAT IS SIN?

Sin is...doing bad things.

Beth, age 6

Listening to the devil and letting him make you do bad things.

Tracey, age 7

Being bad to God.

Linda, age 6

Not following the Ten Commandments.

Lynn, age 6

Lying, stealing, killing, being bad. That's sin.

Mark, age 7

People sin. (How?) By being mean to each other.

Alexander, age 7

People sin by not doing the right thing when they know that what they are doing is wrong.

Haley, age 11

Sin is anything that is not right.

Billy, age 8

I don't know what sin is, but I guess it's like being sassy to your mother or taking things that don't belong to you.

Mark, age 5

Whoever knows what is right to do and fails to do it, for him it is sin.

James 4:17

IF A PERSON SINS AND YOU SEE HIM OR HER, WHAT WOULD YOU DO?

I'd tell him he was bad and
tell him about Jesus.

Kevin, age 8

I'd tell my pastor about him,
and tell him to talk to him
and get him to not do it again,
maybe?

Carolyn, age 7

I'd make him do right, unless
he was a grown-up, then I
couldn't do anything about
it because I'm just a
little kid.

Leroi, age 8

I'd pray for him and ask
God to make him do better.

Charlie, age 8

WHAT DO YOU THINK OF THE DEVIL?

My mother said I looked like the devil. I don't think I look like the devil, do you?

Johnny, age 10

The devil is busy, at least that's what Ms. Dickson says.

Charles, age 9

The devil can beat up on everybody, except God.

Sammy, age 7

The devil is bad!

Alexander, age 6

The devil doesn't like for you to be good.

Marcia, age 6

Be sober, be watchful. Your adversary the devil prowls around like a roaring lion, seeking someone to devour. Resist him, firm in your faith, knowing that the same experience of suffering is required of your brotherhood throughout the world.

1 Peter 5:8

WHICH ONE OF THE TEN COMMANDMENTS DO YOU SEE OTHER PEOPLE BREAKING THE MOST?

They don't love God.

Tim, age 10

I don't know 'cause most people break them all.

Alvin, age 9

People tell stories (lies) **and that's bad.**

Gina, age 7

Working on Sunday is the one people do all the time.

Kevin, age 8

I see people doing bad stuff all the time on the television.

Jeanne, age 7

You shall love the Lord your God with all your heart, and with all your soul, and with all your mind. This is the great and first commandment. And a second is like it, You shall love your neighbor as yourself. On these two commandments depend all the Law and the Prophets.

Matthew 22:37-40

WHAT DOES "TAKING THE LORD'S NAME IN VAIN" MEAN?

To use bad words is swearing.

Charlie, age 8

Cheating on God (is taking the Lord's name in vain).

Seay, age 6

Telling bad things about God (is taking the Lord's name in vain).

April, age 6

Things big people say when they're mad at God. It isn't nice.

Lori, age 6

WHAT IS AN ATHEIST?

That's a person who doesn't
 believe in God.
Lynn, age 12

That's a person who doesn't
 like God and doesn't want
other people to believe in Him.
Willy, age 8

I never heard of a— (atheist).
 Well, whatever; they must not
 be too important because
 Mrs. King (the teacher) hasn't
 taught us about them yet.
Leroi, age 8

Aren't they people who don't
 want people to pray in
       school and stuff?
Paula, age 12

The fool says in his heart, "There is no God." They are corrupt; they do abominable deeds, there is none that does good.

Psalm 14:1

WHAT DO YOU LIKE BEST ABOUT CHURCH SERVICE?

I like the songs. I like to sing, but I don't know the words. Most of the time I just hum.
Lynn, age 5

I like it when everybody sings. I like the way the floor jumps when everybody is singing.
Jason, age 5

My favorite part is when we say the Lord's Prayer. I understand that part. The part you have to read, I can't, 'cause I can't read yet.
Rhonda, age 6

When the preacher says "Amen". That's the best part!
Billy, age 9

I like the organ music. I want to play the organ someday for our church. I play the piano now.
Joyce Lynn, age 9

I like it when we sing...the young people's choir. We only get to sing once a month and at Christmas and Easter. I really enjoy choir practice and Sundays when we sing.
Margie, age 10

God is spirit, and those who worship Him must worship in spirit and truth.

John 4:24

HOW DO YOU PRAY?

I always say the Lord's Prayer, because I remember it. — Billy, age 8

I tell God things that I wouldn't tell anybody else. Is that praying? — Tracey, age 7

I get on my knees and fold my hands and close my eyes. That's how I pray. How do you pray? — Linda, age 6

I pray at night before I go to bed. I say thank you to God, and I ask Him to take care of me and my friends and mother and father. — Pete, age 7

I know lots of prayers. Sometimes I say them at the dinner table and sometimes I say them before I go to bed, and sometimes I say them at church. — Angie, age 7

I pray when I need help, but not all the time. — Bobby, age 8

I pray all the time. — Sammy, age 6

I pray every day and on Sunday at church. — Marcia, age 6

WHAT IS YOUR FAVORITE PRAYER?

My favorite prayer is the 23rd Psalm..."Our Father who art in heaven..."

Charles, age 6

That's not the 23rd Psalm, that's the Lord's Prayer! The 23rd Psalm is "The Lord is my Shepherd I shall not want."

Leroi, age 8

My favorite prayer is "Dear gracious Lord, smile upon us and feed our souls as well our bodies, for Christ's sake, Amen."

Leon, age 8

(Leon weighs over 100 lbs. Everyone sort of chuckled because it was typical of Leon to have a table prayer for a favorite.)

I like the Our Father Prayer.

Angela, age 6

WHAT IS AN ANGEL?

An angel is one of God's friends that lives in heaven.

Pete, age 7

An angel is God's helper.

Grace, age 8

Gabriel is an angel, and there are some more. I don't know who they are, but they fly around and sing and blow trumpets and play harps.

Bobby, age 8

Angels do what God tells them to do.

Johnny, age 10

WHAT IS A MIRACLE?

That's when God makes something really good happen.
Grace, age 8

A miracle is when everybody thinks that something can't happen and it does... or something will happen and it doesn't.
Charles, age 9

I know, isn't that when a person is dying and they don't die?
Pete, age 7

Jesus did miracles, didn't He? (Can you think of one?) He came back alive after He died.
Bobby, age 8

A miracle is a very special something that doesn't happen very often.
Haley, age 11

DO YOU READ THE BIBLE?

Sometimes...
Lynn, age 12

My mom reads it to me sometimes, but not too often.
David, age 8

We read the Bible on Sunday morning at breakfast.
Mike, age 8

I can't read yet, but when I can, I think I will read it.
Hank, age 7

It's too hard to read, and the words are so big.
Mickey, age 7

I don't understand the Bible because they use funny words.
Marsha, age 8

I like my Bible story book because I can read it.
Lonnie, age 8

WHO IS YOUR FAVORITE BIBLE CHARACTER AND WHY?

I Like Moses 'cause he beat the bad guys and got away.
Sammy, age 7

I Like Mary because she reminds me of my mother.
Beth, age 6

I Like Peter because I like to fish, and He was a good friend of Jesus.
Billy, age 8

I Like Samson because he was strong and pushed over a building.
Alexander, age 6

I Like Moses because he gave us the Ten Commandments and talked to God. He and God were good friends, and he did what God told him to do.
Angie, age 7

I Like the boy who ran away. (The prodigal son?) Yes, he ran away and came back home. I wanted to run away one time, but I got scared and didn't do it.
Pete, age 7

FINISH THIS POEM: ROSES ARE RED VIOLETS ARE BLUE GOD IS GREAT AND...

Good to you.

Jean, age 8

Loves you, and you, and you.

Paula, age 8

Jesus, too.

Tracey, age 8

Loves us too.

Tim, age 8

Knows what to do.

Tony, age 8

Loves everybody at school.

David, age 6